Envies the Birds

Envies the Birds

Angelina D'Roza

Longbarrow Press

Published in 2016 by
Longbarrow Press
76 Holme Lane
Sheffield
S6 4JW

www.longbarrowpress.com

Printed by T.J. International Ltd,
Padstow, Cornwall

All rights reserved

Poems © Angelina D'Roza 2016
Jacket artwork and design © Beverley Green 2016

Some of these poems, or versions of poems, have appeared in the following magazines and books, to whose editors I am grateful:
'Days' (*Poetry Review 102: 3*, 2012)
'Memphis Belle' and 'Shifts'
(*The Sheffield Anthology*, Smith|Doorstop, 2012)
'To the Corner Shop and Back', 'Ball Street Bridge'
and 'Stone Walls and Snowgates' (*Iota 92*, 2013)
'The Bench', 'Ball Street Bridge' and 'Stone Walls and Snowgates'
(*The Footing*, Longbarrow Press, 2013)
'Crush' (*Route 57 11*, 2015)
'Stripping for Our Lady of La Salette'
(*Locomotive*, 2016)

ISBN 978-1-906175-29-0

First edition

Contents

9   Song of Silence

10   Definition
11   Onion
12   Stripping for Our Lady of La Salette
13   The Drove

16   Cuttlefish Bones

17   Memphis Belle
18   Crush
20   Youth Training
22   To the Corner Shop and Back
23   Charm for Misspent Youth
24   All Tomorrow's Parties
25   Seventeen
26   Shifts
28   Ada
30   Fairytale No. 9
34   The Lioness in Love

35   Cuttlefish Bones

36   Clockwork
37   Days
38   Aseptic Technique
40   Come the Evening
41   Days
42   Sleep
43   Winter Beds
45   Circles
46   Days
47   Carnations

48	Dawn Chorus
49	The Bench
50	Stone Walls and Snowgates
51	The Mathematician in Love
52	Fairytale No. 13
56	Ball Street Bridge
57	Cuttlefish Bones
58	Postcard
59	Marginalia
63	Dawn Chorus
64	Breech
65	Absent
66	In the Absence of Music
67	Brutal Love
69	Cuttlefish Bones
70	Postcard
71	Darling
72	The Peripatetic in Love
73	Strange Fruit
74	Fairytale No. 16
75	Postcard
77	*Notes*
79	*Acknowledgements*

For Bradley, Dominic and Daniel

no more do we
hide our dreams
we wear them
on our shirts
round our necks
they make music
in our hair

'Darkness Song', Karoniaktatie

Song of Silence

Darkness, my old friend, you old fowl, how charmingly sweet you sing, like silent raindrops. You old foxhole, my old fright, you old fracture. You have a great gift for silence, but I'm no longer able to separate silence from prayer, silk from preamble, old friend, old fragrance. There is no such thing as silence

only the utter and heartbreaking stupidity of words, the utter and heavenly stutter. I have freed myself and remain alone, darkness, darling, my old frill, you old fragment. How charmingly swell you sing, you sing, a procession of basic emptiness, an avalanche, an aviary. Ideas are one thing, silence another.

Definition

1982, my first time round someone else's,
tea with Amy from school. Bucks Fizz sing
in her kitchen. Over the sink, her mum's
peeling potatoes. Her dad shoulders off
his coat and day, same as all the dads,
weather-pink skin, milky in the creases,
words like gritstone warmed in his pockets.

We eat egg, beans and chips from plain
white plates. They settle in for Emmerdale.
I go home with changes Mum should make
and as she kisses me goodnight, I tell her
in my new accent, less spice, no more rice.
I show her under the night-light's glow
my prayer-shaped hands are pale as paper.

Onion

Fluorescent with fake stars, my sister's room
is myth replete with dry ice and rumour.
She is a sprite just out of view, made real by stories
our mother still spins. Little sister copies me
forever wanting the crayon in my hand.
When they give me a microscope, she wants in

while I slice an onion, tweeze a slither onto glass,
try another lens to see stained nucleus.
When I prick my thumb, it's to show her
how blood should look, compare it to her own.
We sit together a long time counting cells
like prayer beads. I remember, and don't remember

any of this. I cut till the air is sharp,
                    repeating myself flawlessly.

Stripping for Our Lady of La Salette

The stream's spilling over the hillside, as the tour guide,
already down to his boxers, points at Our Lady,
her bronze back bent with grief – *She's crying for you,*
he says, *for your sins.* The others strip and immerse
in this cold and holy ravine, dawn-lit strangers baring
penitence to the cows, the alpine birds perched
on low branches, preening their gold-tipped reflection –
they're a comfort against all this belief; how selfish
they seem, seeing only themselves in the water.

*

My sister bathed for Our Lady of Lourdes, quiet as mist
and cancer in her cells, despite our Hail Marys.
I've heard the story often, can't tell what's memory,
what's hearsay: the nun pulling me up to the water –
Watch this lady not making a fuss – a pair of nylons flung
to one side, women wading breast-deep in bathtubs
cut from the rock. I don't believe this icy blessing
can heal, scream when Mum tries my buttons,
fold my arms to my chest, pinning my dress to my body.

*

The water never rests. It's bubbling over the guide's lap
like a burst pipe. He's smiling, waving me in
but how much is alive and fizzing against all that skin?
He's disappointed in me. As they dry out like fish
at the virgin's feet, he fills his flask, urging us to share
for miracle's sake. I don't expect to divine my sister
in the water's lime and sulphates. But let me prove
she's not there, be sure this whole thing's a joke.
I sip and pass the bottle on, wait for nothing to happen.

The Drove

1. Lady-Hare
(*after* Curled *by Sophie Ryder 2009)*

Curled on her side, a long ear cloaks her shoulder
and her arms wrap her knees like ribbon.
Her nose warms her elbow with breath. From here

shadows separate toes, and darkening of thigh
defines her haunch. Counting ribs rise and fall
it's possible to tell how deep the sleep, how happy

the dream. She's not in pain. But see how tight
she holds herself. Is she lonely? She left you
for this quiet place drained of colour and endings.

Aren't you mad at her? She sleeps through,
and you had to fill the gap she made. Compare
the lush fur on her throat – how young she looks –

with your own skin. Why worry about her?
If she misses you let her wake, tell you to your face.

2. The Velveteen Rabbit

Her paw's still sticky with Band-Aid, where the doctor,
a woman in tan sandals – who stopped to thumb the sateen
nap of her inner ear – drew blood. They did everything

to the rabbit first. For the lumbar puncture, they nudged
her beanbag legs up to her belly, and tucked her head
in her dewlap. The betadine swab stained her tail

and if she could talk, she'd have told my sister
the local anaesthetic stings and spreads
like jellyfish under her skin. Her hip's shorn

where they burrowed for marrow; cotton wool strips
straggling the wound, tatty as half-blown dandelion clocks
and brazen with disinfectant – I'm grudging

of how close she was, how in on it all, while I'd to go
to school the next morning, with nothing to say I was there.

3. Nocturne
(after Lady-Hares in a Forest *by Sophie Ryder 1999)*

One year after, a hare moved into her room –
the house smelt of animal, all lick-wet fur and faeces.
We heard her foraging sock drawers at night,

and each morning, strands of jumper smattered
the carpet. We talked about everything but,
while the drum of her paws trembled our lights.

By August, we'd grown so used to her beat,
peace woke me. Wrapped in her empty bedding
I watched her dancing in our backyard,

hares everywhere, up on the slender brawn
of their hinds, like totems blown from their roots.
I'd no business shouting her home or hoping

she'd stay, but I was just then remembering
how hard it is to outrun such unrelenting quiet.

Cuttlefish Bones
After Montale

Don't ask me for words that square
the edge of your ramshackle dreams
and shout your name in fire-lit letters
like a yellow crocus in a dusty field.

You'd be better rambling round town
making friends out of strangers
and not worrying how summer papers
your shadow onto crumbling walls.

Don't ask lyrics to change the world:
a mouthful of gnarled syllables, dry
as branches. All there is to say
is what we're not, what we don't want.

Memphis Belle

You're singing *Danny Boy*
playing tail gunner
as we climb the gennel

skidding the steep slew
of cobbles slippy with rain.

Your fly-by knocks me
and I pretend to mind
your Slush Puppy breath

shrugging you off,
my elbow stoking your ribcage.

I can feel the soft spaces
between your bones
the rub of clothes on your skin.

The hill can't last
and as we near the top

where you turn left and I don't,
I'm dream-slow, heavy
like skies *hushed with snow.*

Behind me the Odeon
floodlights the afternoon

and ahead you stand
expecting me to keep up
or at least stay close.

Crush

Obsess is an ugly word, she says, in the beige
and paper atrophy of 19th Century Fiction.
Marching drums are just turning off Arundel,
slogans blowing in the late May wind

while she flicks between pages of Brontë
and the stairwell, where any minute he might emerge.
I admire her ability to blush, instinctive
as an animal ready to run at the whiff of fox.

                       My skin is inexpressive.
I've heard this makes me hard to read.

*

Not obsessed, then. But to bear one thought
into every room – the thought is a moth
precarious on her thumbnail, wings folded
like pages, no less absurd than when it first settled
harmless as rain.
                    She's fond of the moth,
weighs her movements against the risk of flight,
wrist braced at an angle to lock them eye
to compound eye. Now what if he does emerge
from the stairwell, rushes across the room
to touch her frozen fingers –

will she reciprocate, take his hand
                       and send the moth fluttering?

*

Those marching drums, the clarinetists
with their band camps, their arpeggios, always
a bagatelle to perfect, and no time
between metronome beats for this ill-lit desire
                to what – coexist?

Tomorrow, I'll join the orchestra,
learn cor anglais to fill my head with noise.
I want to be someone else's delusion,
turn tail on their meaningful looks,
                walk home alone

    through low cloud and snickets
thick in morning glory to practice my scales.

Youth Training

i.

They show her how to lift, elbow crook
under an armpit, back straight and on three.
She lowers a man twice her weight

into a lukewarm bath, wrings a flannel
on creased skin, vein-blue, too thin to rub.

ii.

She dips his razor in the cooling water,
asks him to hold still. He tells her he likes Bogart,
the one where they sing the Marseillaise.
His son's name was Peter, after the actor,
his wife's, Grace. They lived in a terrace
near Wadsley, with steep stairs,
a creaky third one up, and a banister
he made from scratch. They'd an indoor toilet
and an attic with boxes, one for LPs –
a Scott Walker and two copies of *Ella Sings
the Blues* went to St Luke's, but they kept
the rest, though the turntable broke in the move –
one box for her china birds, mostly finches
and a chipped heron. Another box for baubles,
bits of tinsel and a plastic baby Jesus
went rotten when the roof leaked.
They listened to Desert Island Discs on Mondays,
Ken Bruce on Tuesdays. They'd three sets, a red one,
one with buttons instead of a dial and one
that only picked up long-wave.
Peter bought them a TV. She had a thing
for Trevor Howard, and a grandchild, he thinks,
but the snow on the set sent her eyes funny
and it's not like going to the pictures.

To the Corner Shop and Back

The old man, with his blue-stripe carrier
and his quarter of spice, skitters in the wind
on the heels of last light. He's searching

for his tower block, block F, with the view
of Claywood Hill, and the windowsill
lined with china birds. He rubs his hands

like flint and steel, buttons his cardigan.
He's stamping out the night when he walks
back and again where his home ought to be.

It should be here, block F, he's sure,
the entrance half-lit where a bulb's blown,
door wedged open with gum in the hinge,

the stairwell linger of tabs and bleach
like wash day on her skin. He's fetched milk
for her tea, she'll not sleep till she's had it.

Charm for Misspent Youth

be to ourselves
children, but we
as children, we

nay we never
and women, when
very little things

be feeling ourselves
asleep, and when
we are weary

thinking, and we
are very men
and old as grown

and be so always
losing ourselves

All Tomorrow's Parties

The backseat is warm, at least, as the bus idles.
Resting her head on juddering Perspex, she pretends
to sleep, that when she looks outside next

there'll be more light than the all-night neon
of the Pennywise Laundrette. And noise. Too early
for birdsong, she listens to Nico's voice vibrating

like a cello string, the certainty of the tambourine.
It's right that this is how the still-dark sounds.
While the bus gears up for the hill home

she hangs on to that last minute; words sink
into a clutter of notes that could suggest hope
but somehow don't, like waking and not knowing

where, or who with. She tidies her hair
behind an ear, rewinds the cassette, listens again.

Seventeen

i.

You're in HMV, reading the back of *Lady
and the Tramp* remastered on VHS, anything
to stop you being early, but the words ravel.
You panic buy, and the guy behind the till

unleashes your free stuffed Lady. None of this
fits your jean pocket – now you've to meet
some boy you kissed in a club, with a children's animation
and soft toy casually wedged under an arm.

ii.

Listening to *Mellon Collie and the Infinite Sadness*
you swap stories under glow-in-the-dark stars
that offer little in dim constellations –

to know the future would be exhausting. Better
to lie there, wrapped to the nines in unmade sheets,
sycamore leaves nodding at his window.

Shifts

Back from the nursing home and locked out,
my keys with the crisps in the fruit bowl.
We don't have mobiles. No one does.
There's a phone box over on Duke Street
but where would I call? I saw my first body

this morning, she was old, of course
so no surprise. She wasn't even one of mine
but I cried to see her yellow cheeks sunk
against bone. They'd took her by twelve.
No hoist, no bed-sized lift. It wasn't funny.

You can picture how we madeshift
getting her downstairs and out the door.
But I'm sitting under the light from our block
waiting to tell you it all, how the matron
was mistaken for a patient by the driver

who ushered her into an armchair. Stowed
in the smoke hole we laughed about that
almost forgetting the death. They said
I've to get used and stop fretting, like it's just
another day. I'll be glad when you're home.

We'll talk about something else, about the night
you locked us both out, keys dropped
in the Penny Black, your shoulder barge
not up to much, and the old bloke from the flat
upstairs taking us in like abandoned puppies

or when we were meant to be out with Vinnie,
babysitter sorted, you cutting it fine in the bath
and me painting my nails huckleberry red.
You never said how it happened, mirror
smashed on the tile, your thumb sliced

like a soft-boiled egg, its bloody yolk
staining the towel. I wasn't much of a nurse
that day either, went to the shop for plasters.
You scarred under butterfly stitches, a slug
thickset and silvering. I know you've seen it

when you St Johned at Hillsborough, but she
was my first, and it must've been worse for you.
But I can help now, with those dreams
you don't have, and whatever impulse it was
made that glass shatter in your hand.

Come home. Or telepath me where you are.
We'll walk back together, your arm round my waist,
my hand in your pocket, warm enough
to stem the sight of her sheet-wrapped face
or the thought of the early shift tomorrow.

Ada

We'd stay forever but the stairs are getting tricky.
Terry from two doors down sits on my two-seater
handed from Auntie Flo to Nan then me
along with the ironing-board for my eighteenth.
His tab-end Park Drive drops ash in his tea
while he tells me about his Ada, how the Social

brought her bed downstairs, jam and butter
a sandwich on Wednesdays, help her dress Fridays.
There'll be a new girl at this place. The letter
he's tapping says they're pleased to inform him
of an opening, but doesn't say who died
to make the room. He's shuffling to the edge

one buttock at a time, his pot gut popping
when he leans head over toes. *We'd stay forever.*
He hoists himself to his slippers, pulls on his coat,
blue-black, thready at the wrist, stretches a hand
in front as he walks, clutching the top of the TV,
the bookcase, the under-the-stairs door handle.

Them bins are on fire again. His eyes nod
to my kitchen, smoke breaking loose through the vent,
fogging the kettle, the bread defrosting on the stove.
Terry scuffs across the landing, turns to wave
as he steps over his own white sill. I can hear Ada
calling for him, her pale pink nighty dark with wet

and half over her head, one loose breast
slipped under her armpit, a mess of talc and Sudocrem.
The key double-locks like brass cogs,
a grandmother clock readying to chime the hour.
A soft shudder underfoot. Water jets hit the bins
like breaking glass. The soot stink of hot nappies

tempers as it cools, straying through pegged sheets,
a stain that carries into the courtyard, past trees,
fallen apples rolled under leaky Escorts,
over the footbridge and grassy ditch where truants
sit and smoke, toke and cough, jeans halfway
down their boxers, playing I Spy for matches.

Fairytale No. 9

i.

A wood grew where my arteries used to,
a devotion of thick, sapful bines pouring
sticky nourishment into muscle.

Heavy with buds, I took to bed, dreamt
of being a woman –
              the weight of nesting birds
on my chest was only grief, the body taking
its share of the pain.
                      I lost my silver bark,
its counter-light reflecting the names
of passersby cut into my ribs.

I missed the birds, the hope of migration,
that in their beakless absence
                I'd unleaf, winter.

ii.

He said his country had only two seasons,
all or nothing, *no spring or fall.*
                He longed to see snow
but I told him how leaves brittle
    and burn up in love for the trees,
sacrifice themselves – little drops of blood –
to lie over exposed roots, warming them
from the early frost.
            Autumn, I said.
Outside, sand and sky were all one colour.
He turned back from the still heat
asked me to write
        this new word on his hand.

iii.

Rising out of long-spun sleep, I ran childish
            and bare-legged, roared
with the Porter as it cut its rainy way
from sedge grass moors to Hunters Bar –
crest-foam spewed,
              flung sticklebacks townwards.

It took more earth for itself, worrying
the embankment's edge. One weak spot
the river's silver would burst its seam.

Now in nothing but dry light, I forget
the crystal-cold that comes with blue sky,
            step outdoors expecting
this autumn's echo of summer sun
                      to keep its word

but this pale shine is all show.
It keeps me awake, and I am illuminated
to distraction,
      have no use for these clear days.

iv.

Not an amputation with its careful stitches
mapping what's gone in bright scars.
                  Her feet are still here, but numb
as if a wall where her body used to end
crumbled from too much touch –

hands, tongue, lapping like salt-spray –

and all herself is leaking into the ground.
Good for the ground. Geraniums
              and begonia are blossoming.
She tries to shore her wounds
with spit-softened soil, the way mothers
finger-feed the runt in their brood.

Dead to the world, her skin will outlast her
   like a blown eggshell or empty room
but she'll get so far with this makeshift mentality.
Better than waiting to be saved.
                      And no, that quiet
as she sucks dirt from under her nails
   is not strength. Not yet.

The Lioness in Love
After Aesop

That night the lioness fell apart for a dream, demanded to marry it.
The dream was not impressed, but the lioness, furious with desire,
threatened a kiss, and the dream realised such a mouth
was not to be denied. He said, "I'm flattered by your prose.
But what great noise you have!
                              What great craving! Where is the dream
that wouldn't be frightened? You must have your noise pulled out
and your craving pared before you can be a moon for me."

And what won't a lioness do for love? If she'd read the fable
she'd have seen the dream's trick coming, but tried for him anyway.
So would you. She's out there now, warm and unsatisfied
and no less in love. That's the lesson. Of course, this is only a story
and the lioness only human, but watch her noise grow back
      as she pounds the woods, the musculature of bare shoulders
revealing the mettle that got her this far, wherever this far is.

Cuttlefish Bones
After Montale

Midday-pale and dazed, he rests
in a scant shadow of scorched trellis,
his mind elsewhere. Thorns snap

under the weight of blackbird;
sweetbrier bristles with snakes.
In cracked soil, or pacing the vetch

rows of red ants break, now dovetail,
as they scale sheaves of stalks.
And shy between pine branches

the steel-drum sea beats; cicada
rattle-songs roll down crags.
He ambles back into day's dazzle,

heavy with wonder – all life's care
and sweat trails this rose trellis, edged
with emeralds of broken bottle.

Clockwork

We stare through ribs and pneumonia,
x-rays held to the partial eclipse,
and let the morning's long words drift
like paper boats, the Latin for bones
and breath. This is our last shift
as student nurses – we huddle
on the fire-escape, door wedged open
with oxygen: a sputter of nightingales
under a negative sky. We know
the intricacies of the body
its musculature, can describe
the impulse of your heart,
read its flicker on ultrasound.
I've learnt to locate a twelve-week foetus
through an almost swollen stomach,
to find the pubic bone,
palpate the uterus under pressure
of full bladder. So much is weighted
against that nut of cells.
The clouds let slip bruised light
as something the black of a tombstone
rolls over the sun, revealing
the workings of Earth, so for this minute
of upturned pause, nothing is wasted.

Days

It always comes down to this one early,
one patient and his Polish, his dementia,
the way his emaciating body founders
in the mattress pooling with faecal fluid

spilling from his stomach, the stoma bag
blown off, small intestine poking through,
a blooming crimson rose warm to the touch.

We look across the bed to one another
inadequate in aprons and gloves, soapy water
turning cold as we wonder where to begin,
then wade in, wrist deep and reassuring,

forgetting the intimacy, the oddness of it all,
our fingers reading ribs and ruckled scar,
a quiet language persisting between us.

Aseptic Technique

Cars pull up at the rain-shined entrance
where the road-river silvers from the drain
and an ambulance tailgate unloads

the oxygen, the smoker still wearing slippers
clutching the remote. Neon above sliding doors
reads *Emergencies*, the *Em* strobing

like it's 1989 and nothing's changed
since the nurses' white origami halos
sterile and hair-gripped, or the sister's habit

of pocketing painkillers home for her mother
when her legs swelled up, ulcerating,
the smell of pustulating skin and fat

that hung in the air like washing.
On the fire stairs Maggie stubs her smoke
into the Quality Street tin lid

pulls her pink towelling dressing-gown tight
and drags her drip-stand back to bed
for 10 o'clock drugs. She won't sleep.

In the bed next to hers, curtains pulled,
gurgled wheezing crawls the walls like mildew
until 4:15 when it stops.

Low voices and chair legs scrape
the buffed-raw linoleum
as relatives void into the lobby.

Working his collar loose, the chaplain
dumps his body in the canteen
with the sitting stench of peas and colostomies.

He won't go home to the hollowed cheeks
of his sleeping wife until he has to.
He has to be there when she wakes

when temazepam and morphine wear thin
and daylight breaks her eyelids' papery windows.
6am, the sun's on her face as Maggie showers

and gowns for theatre, checklist ticked
no false teeth, no pregnancy, wedding ring removed.
She's tucked between the white, cuffed sheet

and hard white pillow like an expectant statue
as Sister steps through the sliding doors
and into the road still wet with rain.

Come the Evening

He hooks his thumb in the loose knot of his wife's hand.
She unnests her head from her arms,
hisses a spray of thick saliva. Her gown's off the shoulder
revealing skin, candle-white and pocked with scars –
an opiate patch picked like a scab:
        Nurse, she'll not let me change it. Can you try?
I wash and glove up. She breathes in;
her ribs lift an inch. I tell her it won't hurt.
                                      She bats me off.
Third go, her strength musters in a clammy fist.
She slurs obscenities, thinks I'm after her purse,
        says she's expecting her husband any minute.

He hushes me out of the way and into a visitor's chair.

Days

It always comes down to this one early,
the way his emaciating body founders,
a blooming crimson rose warm to the touch,
turning cold as we wonder where to begin –

one patient and his Polish, his dementia,
in the mattress pooling with faecal fluid,
our fingers reading ribs and ruckled scar

blown open, small intestine poking through,
spilling from his stomach, the stoma.
Inadequate in aprons, gloves, soapy water
we look across the bed to one another,

a quiet language persisting between us,
forget the intimacy, the oddness of it all,
then wade in, wrist deep and reassuring.

Sleep

Shrouded in her
deepest fissure
purple poppies

crouch sighing
in snowmelt,
petals draped

from stalks
like sleeping limbs
sprawling naked.

Palpating a bine
of sluggish vein
I pull tight

the tourniquet.
Narcan spews
from the syringe

and smacks
her placid blood
kicking the lungs

from their opiate-
deep and almost
breathless sleep.

Winter Beds

Mid-December through hospital windows
low noon light prickles where frost's clung
to woods butting the road behind Urology.

What I saw in this view,
            in the off-white, sterile distance
those years I worked here, I don't know.

We all looked out to the trees for something
as we counted heartbeats and breaths –
for some, the promise of uncertain weather,

a sudden ice in the air, a plush of rainfall
between branches.
                But a nurse who walked

away from the ward was only evoked
in hushed tones, storeroom door pulled-to
as though we were naming our dead.

                Did they talk about me
the months after I left? No longer in uniform,
sitting in my bed, oxygen mask like a charm

strung from my neck, I miss the musk and pelt
of the undergrowth, the coarse winter wind
scouring my lungs.

*

She asks and I tell her, *Sister,*
wintering out there I'm no less a nurse
than walking the ward, gloves on, pocketful

of stethoscope. She wears her navy blue
like a cat wears fur, her nurse-ness warm
in its seams, sung in the rustle of polyester.

I carry the drip rate equation in my mouth
and the names of major veins flit the tips
of my thumbs like waxwings on a holly bush.

She turns my hands over in hers, a flutter
of scrubbed red – with her first two fingers
resting on my wrist, she asks again.

*

Tonight when they flick out the lights,
the dark of the ward makes the woods bright,
an icy mirror reflecting back

                               my face in the branches.
And in the wooze of post-anaesthesia
I can't tell whether I'm here or out there

letting my skin numb in the snow –
       under the long frayed shadows of oaks
and drip-stands, I dream

I'm walking from bay to bay, measuring
pain, changing sheets, looking to the trees
             as patients turn in their sleep.

Circles

The doctor slides the diagram to me. It's not art
though some of the circles drift like balloons.
He's waiting for me to see what he sees, chin tipped,
silverlit in the hot fluorescence of the anglepoise.
I must see it; I've sat the right side of this bed,
best nurse's face on, watching doctors deliver bad news,
leaning forwards, elbows on knees for the slow build,
working the woman, who fidgets in her gown
(I watch myself fidget in my gown), crossing, uncrossing
pale-veined legs, tugging the yellow trim
of our flimsy hospital threads. The clinical air
prickles our back where the gown gapes
and our bra ought to be. By the time he tells us
we already know, we're not pulling through this intact.

Words now, lots of them, his tongue like an eel
flicking the back of his teeth. Moss-green rose-heads
on the curtains closed round us are massive
behind his small face. If we can touch
those swollen petals we could walk out, leave him
with his news, his treatment plan, his circles
and cell mutation. But we're pinned by the chewed
end of his pen pointed at the scrap of paper mapping
the abnormal tissue inside us. We sip the plastic
glass of ice-melt, set it back on the table
careful to match its wet base with the water-ring.
He rises and folds our notes under his arm
tucking them into a wheel of shirt-sweat,
shakes our hand. We nod as though we understand.

Days

A quiet language persisting between us,
our fingers reading ribs and ruckled scar,
we forget the intimacy, the oddness of it all
then wade in, wrist deep and reassuring,

turn cold as we wonder where to begin,
inadequate in aprons, gloves, soapy water.
We look across the bed to one another –

a blooming crimson rose warm to the touch,
sawn-off small intestine poking through,
spilling from his stomach, the stoma bag
in the mattress pooling with faecal fluid.

The way his emaciating body founders,
this one patient and his Polish, his dementia –
it always comes down to this one early.

Carnations

In your dressing gown, no mascara
your pale lashes are more naked

than all the bodies I've seen on wards.
I stroke your breast's cratered edge

with saline-soaked cotton, until pink
raw mammary glints like carnations

after rain, fresh cut from the park
as though I'm late for tea and sorry.

Dawn Chorus

i.

Lament the morning,
bullfinch, bemoan its brittle
light so shy and cold

ii.

chip-chip-chip-tell-tell
tell-cherry-erry-erry
tissy-che-wee-ooo

The Bench

On these moss-wet slats
a stranger's name is carved above the inscription
*One touch of nature makes
the whole world kin.*   My remembering's
a bus across town, so I sit here, borrow
someone else's dead.
                          What do they think
when they think about you
and this perishable view everywhere –

leaves everywhere   bracken and oak
like broken bones on the bluish path,
turtle-green tapers scorched to brass, spirals
of snuffed candle smoke.

I snatch sight of you, stranger,
flame of blue-tipped bird skulking
the underbrush   thistled between glances.

             You crouch in my unhatted head
with your trowel and samples, a mote
of sloughed-off skin in my eye   making me
name the breed of an egg
by its weight in my hand, the Latin
                          for all these leaves.
       I conjure you
from falling flecks of image and dust –
             the black cloud of your hair fills
the sky to a storm, as if you're up there and not
       hands and knees in the earth.

Stone Walls and Snowgates

An angler wades in   teetering like a goose
slips on loose silt
                      churned by the Don.
Water rushes past and round him   hip high
      November cold.

The crack willow's ready to tip.
Browning catkins loom on the water.
White geese play in its shallow roots

far from the furnace
              the fire and soot.
                              Only the splash
of red-brick rubble   a broken bumper
                        stuck in the rushes
lets slip the road, the way this river
burst its banks after rain, reached up
        to these stone walls and snowgates
and had a good look at the streets
laced grey with industry   sloped home
with sewage
                and steel dust in its stomach.

He baits his hook and casts to the current
      waits for barbel to bite
in the echo of the gas bell
    the ore-brown walls of Tommy Wards
        the tinny crash of the weir.

The Mathematician in Love

She's out counting cow-lonely gritstone peaks,
dawn-lit and slow along the Edale road,
subtracts his age from the number of hours

she's spent walking, divides by two,

maps equations on the back of her hand
to understand the principles of attraction
but keeps coming back to the one belief she holds –
the simplest answer is probably true

like *The Sound of Someone You Love Who's Going Away*

and It Doesn't Matter, the inescapable songspan
eleven minutes and forty-seven seconds
reliable as Pythagoras. She measures
her steps against its rhythm, passes a lamb
dead on the shaded upslope of Win Hill

and blowflies seduced by what must rot
buzzing six inches above the obtuse angle
of neck-wool and blood. She keeps walking,
divining gradient by chord progression, multiplies
missed calls by time signature. Others descend
as she's climbing, unaware the desire to fall
is inevitable. The answer is at the top
where probability reaches in all directions
and every path leads the way down.

Fairytale No. 13

i.

Blessed is she
who washes her hair
in the Rivelin

who believes
in the rush of the weir
after rain

where the white
bellies of the minnow
are flat and round

as communion.
Blessed is she
who misremembers

how she got here.
She will inherit
the sea.

ii.

In the corner of the pub, I tell you the worst thing about myself, and you, in your green sweatshirt and my imagination, tell me everyone's done that, say ten *Our Fathers*, one *Glory Be*, walk out on the history of home, the sanctity of unchange, walk across rivers the depth of 4am that preach insomnia and lead to temptation.

iii.

The winter life bluebells away and with it
all sense of sanctuary. But safety's for the suburbs,
the ho-hum and goatish. I believe in one divine
and aphoristic fall. I believe in falling often.

iv.

Forgive me
        whoever, I'm trailing
                impure thoughts
                        along the river
                                like bindweed.

Ball Street Bridge

Past the cutlers, halfway over the Don
I stop to watch the river's dull pewter
slow-shimmy the strait, grinding stone,
cutting shingle. Mallards perch the weir

sloped in water-gush and slugs of rain
like dregs of Kelham Ale. I envy their grit,
webbed roots dug down against the braid
of ore-heavy stream, a quiet unshifting.

With moonrise, light pivots as it fails.
The suds beneath glint with gudgeon
and coltsfoot smoulders the watery soil,
yellows the banks like fire. I want to learn

this knack of standing still while headwaters,
washing past, whittle rocks to quartz.

Cuttlefish Bones
After Montale

When I picture your smile, it is clear water,
a pool I catch sight of along the rocky riverbed.
It's a mirror where ivy admires her autumn flowers
under the safety of the white and quiet sky.

I remember this. But I can't say, from so far off,
whether your look lets slip a wide-eyed soul
or if you're another wanderer the world wears thin
who hauls his pain with him like a rabbit's foot.

I can tell you this – that the thought of your face
floods all heartache with calm waves
and that your image creeps into my grey memory
bright as the crown of a young palm...

Postcard

Elevator music pumps
poolside, deranged percussion

vocals forgettable
except this one riff –

even these Persian
almost-magpies repeat

the same few notes
insisting like haze heavy

greenblue moontides
or you: is it 3000 miles?

More? And you came
this far just to sit

in my brain like a song
I can't finish.

Marginalia

i.

In Tibetan, *shul* is the impression left after whatever made it has gone. Stretchmarks. Tan-lines. The reputed guilt of a Catholic childhood. She heard this from her therapist, an imaginary man up Nether Edge, who waters never-never plants and talks in her sleep. He trails Issey Miyake where he walks back and to in front of the giant bay window, no snow or tangerines, only Prokofiev, while he listens to her quiet. This quiet is more *shul* than nothingness and must be given due respect. She thinks it's like the grass on Lose Hill, that doesn't muddy where others have been, but tilts gold at certain times of day, and leads her down from the top. Her therapist doesn't see it. Puts faith in etymology and diet. He perseveres. His voice still sounds when the words stop, a medicinal humming, humming. *Shul.* She's grateful for this language that names the silent weight of you.

ii.

Your handprint, for example. She feels the pressure of fingertips between ribs, a palm on her stomach. When she undresses, she waits for the smell of skin not hers, then folds herself into bed, careful to leave space for an arm, a shoulder.

iii.

Darling – I love these velvet nightlights. I lullaby these nightingales. Darling – I luck these velvet nights. I've never been able to decide… whether I luck you most in the eternal half-light-years that blindfold with deadbeats or in the full fanlight of migration. Or perhaps in the lux of noon. Anyway, I luck you most – I luminous you most – and you phoned me just because you phoned me tonight – I walked on those telling wits for two hourglasses after holding your luck like parentheses to balance me.

iv.

She sits through all the gradations of light. They are thirty-eight, by her count. She disregards melancholy as self-reflexive, like the woman who names herself in her number of great loves. Lamp-light, too. She's seen the desert, where day is only off or on. Except once at 4am, when everything was blue. She tells her therapist so. He leans in like a crack willow seeking sunshine, asks about all that dazzles, but she tells him the moon there wanes from head to toe. None of this side-to-side equivocation. Tonight the light over her garden is a TV that won't turn off. It is fairy stories and reruns of Blind Date, its afterglow burnt on the inside of her eyelids.

v.

Crouched at the foot of the Cholera Monument, she feels its solidity against her back. This must be why she came here as a child, to rest against something more sure than herself, to look on the city shrunk to a manageable size. The council flats of Claywood that hid her are gone, but a tarmac blueprint remembers – the ground unmoved to grow anything new.

vi.

She looks in the mirror, is trying to read her face backwards. Your writing was always beautiful, if hard to take. She traces the words across her collarbone, the marginalia of her throat, onto antique paper like a school project, one of those brass-rubbing, flower-press days, where teaching is somewhere deep in the process, not at all what she thought she'd learn – She creases the paper in half, doesn't know where to send it.

vii.

Darling – our fairyland is almost ended, our falsity, our falsetto tambourine – I'm so sorry for all the miserable misapprehensions, the tinctures, the tinderboxes, for all the miserable miracles I've caused you when we could have been so happy. Darling – our faith, our faithful, our fallacy is almost ended. I think our lifetime together will be like these last three deadbeats – I wish you. I witness you. I wolf you – I'm not afraid of anything.

Dawn Chorus

i.

The backyard's fledging;
rhododendrons groan, heavy
with rain and blackbird

ii.

House sparrow, whittle
the smutty town air until
your whistle runs clear

Breech

The phone burrs in the bedroom
barely there above the clatter of bins

the throaty caw of pied whites
nursing their squab in our chimney.

I press the handset to my ear.
An eggshell frost on the skylight

mutes the morning's rash of blue
and seeps inside the sill.

I bury my head in your chest.
You ask and I tell in ruptured words

reluctant to give the news breath.
In the kitchen our son eats Frosties

pulls on muddied school shoes
his new coat, and calls out, *I'm ready.*

Absent

Notice the morning
stretch and sag
like postpartum skin

how its frail sunlight
lends its warmth
to this intimate view

of sky and branches
plucked bare
blue as newborn flesh

In the Absence of Music

Sunday afternoons, our house drops
to a wheeze; the wind's in every fissure
and empty room, breathing in our dust,
playing us like a bed of reeds. We battle
with this aria, quiet as the cold light
peeping through lowered slats.
We turn up the radio, add the DJ's voice
to our own. And when the house
still deafens us we stroll past front garden
buddleia, trampolines upturned
to keep off rain and strays, to the park
where hawthorn ripens in the borders.
The climbing net bristles with kids
in its bines. November-swept
they natter as the soft earth brittles
and slugs bunk in frost-licked leaves.
Boys swing from monkey bars, make good
their escape as sharks nip their heels.
It is hard not to watch the small girl
in sabbath-pink and patent leather,
white tights mud-black, her skirt tucked
as she clambers the rope to reach
her brother, who bats her off like a fly.
You lean towards me as though to speak.
In ones or twos they are called indoors
until it's just us and the swings,
chain links clinking as the wind catches.

Brutal Love

Springsteen played Bramall Lane
on a July evening much like this – one of those
blond-lit, cut-grass memories – chasing bees
in the garden, while Bruce holds the neighbourhood
in syncopation. Mum's cooking mince and onion
the smell of it like warm breath exhaling
from the back porch. I don't hear the car door
clunk-to on the drive, only the strum,
Tunnel of Love so loud its beat's a second pulse
in my pubescent ribcage. Another encore,
Born to Run extending into my broken sleep.

If I tell you about the car on the drive, clean
and glinting in the tea-time light, and if I let
the sound of its door ticking shut back in,
I've to tell you how the slightest noise
could wake me sweating under two t-shirts,
pyjamas, jumper – that sleeping in my training bra
creased the skin under the small bulge
of my breasts, how I'd creep to the bathroom
testing floorboards, to wash the night from my face –
if I tell you what lying in bed was like
when the music went quiet, the floodlights dark –

I was old by eighteen, worn through like a boot
and on to the next generation. Green Day
played as I tried to breastfeed with bloody
nipples and a son who wouldn't latch.
You were sixty miles away, revising maths to *Dookie*,
daydreaming about that girl in class
wondering if she'd be your first. I didn't wonder
about anything, only woke and fed
and slept, and played my cassettes over
and again like a child. My son would think these songs
lullabies, recite lyrics like bedtime prayers.

He's eighteen now, and a few yards ahead
bouncing with the crowd to *American Idiot* – you say
you can see his hands in the air, and we
in vintage Green Day t-shirts, bounce with him.
We've been dancing in front of this punk-pop altar
for hours, and I am getting younger
with every note. Phones flicker like candles
as the mass slows to *Brutal Love*, the last song.
If we could stay inside this confusion
of bodies, we'd be safe, keep dancing
under the lights, like safety's what we wanted.

Cuttlefish Bones
After Montale

My life, I won't ask for unshakeable
forms, enduring faces or possessions.
Here in your toss and turn, honey
and absinthe taste the same.

A heart that shies from every hurtle
and fall is sometimes startled
the way now, or maybe now, the quiet
of the peaks rings with gunfire.

Postcard

Five to midnight
on the watery edge

of a whitewinter
New Year desert

I could almost
mistake this saveme-

some light for salt,
bread, home.

Darling

Don't try so hard to convince me that you're very old peppermint who's lost his most precious possibility. You really haven't found it yet.

She stands in front of the walls, windows, eyes closed, to think about the present, or whatever it is she thinks about when she's standing, waiting for nothing. There is never nothing. One of those imagined conversations, perhaps. Or the song that blocks it out.

All the firecracker and sweetness, the fire and swell – all the emotional striptease we're capable of is growing – and just because sanity and witch-hunt are growing too and we're building our luck on a fistful of foxgloves, nothing is lost – Darling. Don't try so hard to forget me. Fire. Fire-eater and sweetness – don't try so hard.

Or the lovers who walk from opposite ends of the Great Wall, from the dragon's tail and Yellow Sea, walking, winding, rising and falling towards each other.

The thistles that went to make us are tremendously alive. Don't mourn for a poor little wonderful merry-go-round mentality, because I know I luck you. I lullaby you.

When they meet it will be a parting, a place to say goodbye, to leave, every step smaller than the last.

Because I know I lover you – and you'll come in January to tell me that you do, and we won't wound anymore about anything.

The Peripatetic in Love

Lightning-hearted I take to the roam, the wound and all healing ahead. The East is enough, its distance and distances. I aspire to the instability of sand, its disobedience, how it runs away from the present the way light does. I'm reading about Eskimos, how they walk a straight line east to scatter their anger on the plain, then go home to their lover, their dinner. Their fundamental sense of purpose. I walk the line. I walk on the wild side, sugar. I walk to scatter my wishes through wild grass and up to my armpits in cow parsley, the path entirely lost in this green and sentient lush. No one returns the same way. The rain is an upturned well for the wants you don't know you have. I am filled with them. I walk towards them. Like a nightingale, I migrate at night, and the males sing too late to call me down from the sky. I go too far to hope of return, if hope is what this feeling is.

Strange Fruit

Magnolias, the beauty of those sweet, fresh flowers giving way to violence. I listen alone to those fragile flowers iconic with open mouth. I'm listening to Billie then Nina. I'm watching *Gone with the Wind*. Everyone loves Scarlett. No one likes Scarlett. It's a Saturday, the hottest day of the year outside, but I have nothing to offer in return, so I am watching *Gone with the Wind*. In an hour, Scarlett will vow never to be hungry again. I am not hungry. The news is on the radio, but I like my news past. Ashley is going to war. Ashley is marrying Melanie. He is the ratio of the circumference of the South to its diameter. We never talked about solitude, the comfort of listening to Nina alone, the dangers of listening alone. I believe songs can change everything. I believe in the power of the perfect fifth. I listen alone. I don't believe songs can change the world. Take the inevitability of that last sung note, how the end can't be undone with an unresolved chord. A key change might be enough to postpone some endings. A trumpet solo, or silence, delays another refrain. But who wants that when crows will pluck regardless? Sherman is marching on Charleston. We never talked about cause. Ashley has his cause, Scarlett hers. I am between causes. I go out to celebrate someone else's, thirty years married. Ashley and Melanie won't last so long. I make good conversation with strangers. They are good people. I can tell from their head tilt, their ease in the room. I dance to hide my unease in the room. It's the hottest day of the year outside, Sunday, day of the world without end, of the word everlasting, and I am eating hot cross buns out of season. I'm watching *Gone with the Wind*. It's easier to watch a film knowing how it ends. I have never got to the end. I listen to Siouxsie Sioux. Then Billie, then Nina. The needle resets itself. Magnolias give way. Show me how this ends, this infatuation with the last note, a song-long desire.

Fairytale No. 16
After Aesop

The tortoise at last looks up
envies the birds.

That was the day we climbed Mam Tor. Gabriella blistered her heels and flirted with a man in a glider, who was probably waving back through the sunshine bouncing off his tinted dome of cockpit. She's on tiptoe, hand upstretched, her soft underarm skin exposed, waving like a schoolgirl to the glider, the man, the sky, and we're that close, in vest tops, lit with sweat, watching him smooth down the one cloud, easy as, I think if I could just get up there, catch on the wing, let go over the Hope Valley… Gabriella says *maybe*. But she has a thing for pilots. I have a thing for heights.

I hollow my bones with spoons,
one of those sets for measuring sugar.
The tablespoon works my sternum
but my collarbone, the bones in my wrists,

only take the quarter teaspoon.
You dig out each of my vertebrae,
the heart of my pelvis, for weeks
my marrow under your nails.

Another man tied himself to a hundred helium balloons today, set himself sail over Glossop. They are not all red like the song. Or blue like the ones along the Berlin Wall. I love balloons let go: the South Koreans sending news north, or Maori kites flying letters to the gods. Sometimes I think about this when I think about you. So much depends on wind speed, direction. I watch the footage, mute the commentary trying to predict (a), when he'll land, and (b), where.

Postcard

…to find the greenly
blue day turned red

by sunrise and sandstorm
all the earth lifted

and spun to new shapes
and this smallest

of seabirds undone
from its burrowed

desert crag like some
living Lucy – don't ask

me how its song goes
it will not translate.

Notes

1. The **epigraph** ('no more do we / hide our dreams...') is taken from 'Darkness Song' by Alex Jacobs (Karoniaktatie), *Akwesasne Notes* 5, 5 (Early Autumn, 1973), reprinted in *American Indian Prose and Poetry: We Wait in the Darkness*, ed. by Gloria Levitas, Frank Robert Vivelo, and Jacqueline J. Vivelo.

2. **Song of Silence** takes source texts from Simon & Garfunkel, Edward Lear, Arthur Conan Doyle, Sara Maitland, William Faulkner, P. J. Harvey and John Cage.

3. All poems from Montale's **Cuttlefish Bones** use Jonathan Galassi's *Complete Poems – 1920-1954 Revised Bilingual Edition* (FSG: 2000) and *Montale in English* (ed. Harry Thomas. Handsel: 2005) as starting points.

4. **Charm for Misspent Youth** uses a prose passage from Gertrude Stein's 1925 novel, *The Making of Americans*, as source text.

5. The first stanza of **The Lioness in Love** is adapted from Aesop's "The Lion in Love" (*Aesop's Fables* ed. Jack Zipes. Penguin: 1996).

6. **Dawn Chorus** uses a phonetic rendering of the chaffinch from Tim Birkhead's *The Wisdom of Birds* (Bloomsbury: 2008).

7. The stanzas in **The Mathematician in Love** represent pi to 5 decimal places. This isn't important, but it pleases me.

8. **Marginalia** – Rebecca Solnit talks about *shul* in her book *A Field Guide To Getting Lost* (Canongate Books: 2006). Parts iii. and vii. use the letters of Zelda Sayre to F. Scott Fitzgerald as source text. (*Dear Scott, Dearest Zelda: The love letters of F. Scott & Zelda Fitzgerald*, eds. Jackson R. Bryer & Cathy W. Barks. Bloomsbury: 2002.)

9. **Darling** adapts text from Zelda Sayre's letters and a 1988 film by Marina Abramovic and Ulay, *The Lovers (The Great Wall: Lovers at the Brink)*. A review of Abramovic by Adrian Searle (*The Guardian*, 18 July 2014) lends the sentence: "to stand in front of the walls and windows, where we stood, eyes closed, to think about the present, or whatever it is we think about when we are standing, waiting for nothing. There is never nothing, always something."

10. **The Peripatetic in Love** – The opening two sentences are adapted from Walt Whitman's "Song of the Open Road". And there's something about the Eskimo custom of walking off their anger, by Lucy Lippard, in Rebecca Solnit's *Wanderlust* (Granta 2002). "I walk the line" – Johnny Cash, and "I walk on the wild side, sugar" – Lou Reed. The path where no one returns the same way, and the unconscious desires, is a reference to Tarkovsky's *Stalker*. Chris Watson wrote an article for *The Guardian*, "The echoes of Benjamin Britten's 'composing walks'" (30 January 2013), about listening to Britten and field recordings of birdsong. I read the thing about nightingales there: "Female nightingales migrate at night, and the males sing to call them down out of the sky."

11. **Strange Fruit** – I was reading an article in *The Guardian*, by Anita Sethi (23 June 2015), "Records from a rented room: 'The tragedy of Billie Holiday's life gives her songs pathos'", and the line about magnolias giving way to violence comes from there: "the beauty of those sweet, fresh flowers giving way to the ugliness of violence."

12. The text in quotation marks on the dust jacket ("the channel worn through rock where a river runs in flood, the indentation in the grass where an animal slept last night") is a definition of the word *shul* by a 14th century Tibetan sage (cited in Rebecca Solnit's *A Field Guide To Getting Lost*; see note 8).

Acknowledgements

Two of the **Dawn Chorus** haiku featured in *Call & Response*, a project curated by Paul Evans and Brian Lewis in 2012.

The first two poems from **Cuttlefish Bones** appeared in collaborative exhibitions with Liz Searle at Bank Street Arts, Sheffield, in 2013 and 2014 (the second poem as part of the Midsummer Poetry Festival).

Definition featured in an exhibition at the Royal Festival Hall, Southbank Centre, London, as part of the 2014 *Poetry International* Festival.

Fairytale No. 9 developed as part of a collaboration with the artist Beverley Green. The poems and artwork were exhibited at Bank Street Arts, Sheffield, in May 2015, to coincide with the South Yorkshire Poetry Festival.